COME LEARN WITH ME

The Kingdoms of Life:
Classification

Text by Bridget Anderson

BANK STREET COLLEGE OF EDUCATION
in association with the
AMERICAN MUSEUM OF NATURAL HISTORY
for Lickle Publishing Inc

First published in 2003 by

LICKLE PUBLISHING INC

Library of Congress Control Number

2002113576

ISBN: 1-890674-17-6

ILLUSTRATION AND PHOTO CREDITS

Alaska Forest Association, Ketchikan, Alaska 35r; American Museum of Natural History: 2bl, 2tr, 3br, 11tl, 11tr, 14cl, 14bc, 17, 20tl, 20cl, 20bl, 23br, 25bl, 25tr, 28tr, 29tl, 29cr, 29br, 34bc, 34br, 39bl, 40l, 41tl, 41br, 42-43, 43c, 44tl, 44tr, 44-45b 45t, 45cr—AMNH photographers O. Bauer 11bl; C. Bogert 43t; B.J. Kaston 42cl; Frank Puza 38l, 39tl; B.G. Read 41tr, 41b; R.G. Zweifel 40br; American Phytopathological Society, St. Paul, MN, Reprinted, with permission, from *Compendium of Potato Diseases, 2nd edition*, 2001 27tr; B. Anderson 11, 18-19; Colin Bates 26tr, 26br; Dee Breger, Lamont-Doherty Earth Observatory26 bl; Closetcreations.com, Bermuda 6tr;   Columbia University Libraries, photographer Kari R. Smith, 7b; Crate and Barrel 6bl; Michael Davidson, Molecular Expressions 14tr, 15tr, 23tr; Paul G. Davison, University of North Alabama 31br; Frank Dazzo, Center for Micobial Ecology, Michigan State University 23bl; Stephen Durr 2-3t, 22tr, 24, 25tl; Wim van Egmond 26tl; Garden Club of Palm Beach 12bl, 30tr, 36t, 37tr; George C. Page Museum 42t; Pamela J. W. Gore, Georgia Perimeter College 38br; Elizabeth Gibbs 12tc, 12tr; Nancy Gray 15 cr; William Hahn, Department of Ecology, Evolution, and Environmental Biology, Center for Environmental Research and Conservation, Columbia University 12bc, 12br, 29bl, 30, 31cl, 31cr, 34cr, 35br, 36l; Alan Hale 31tr; Richard T. Hanlin, Georgia Museum of Natural History, University of Georgia 11c; Honnold/Mudd Library, Claremont University Consortium, Claremont, California 7c; Cait Hutnik 43b; Chris Kjeldsen, Sonoma State University 26cr; Everly Conway de Macario and Alberto Macario 2tl, 21b; NASA/JPL/Caltech, courtesy of, 8; National Institutes of Health 14cr; National Oceanic and Atmospheric Administration (NOAA) Photo Library 12t, 20br; National Park Service, Yellowstone National Park 21cl; National Park Service, Redwood National and State Parks 33bl, 37b; Fred Rhoades 27cl, 27br; Sarah Spaulding 22bl; University of California Board of Regents, used with permission: Suzanne Paisley 39c; University of Rhode Island Cooperative Extension 7; USDA-ARS 28, 33r, 34; U.S. Fish and Wildlife Service 2-3, 9tcr, 35cl, 35c, 35cr; USGS, photographer Doyle Stephens 21tr;
John Walker 1
Illustrations: Chris Forsey 13, 16bl, 32; Nancy Heim 37b

Series Director: Charles Davey LLC, New York
Text by Bank Street College of Education:
Andrea Perelman, Project Manager; Elisabeth Jakab, Project Editor
Photographs unless otherwise credited from the American Museum of Natural History:
Maron L. Waxman, Editorial Director; Eric Brothers, Scientific Consultant
Art Direction, Production & Design: Charles Davey *design* LLC
Photo research: Erin Barnett

Printed in China

CONTENTS

The Naming Game

Did you ever notice how everything around you has a name? You sit in a "chair" reading a "book" next to a "lamp." When you first meet someone, you ask "What's your name?" People have always made sense of the world by identifying the things around them. To name something is to know it in some way. Every time you see a chair, you recognize it as a "chair." And because other people also know what a chair is, you can communicate about it with them.

People organize the things in their lives. For example, your clothes are organized in a closet.

Most people would agree that a "chair" is a human-made object for one person to sit on.

But there are so many things to name! To remember them all, people have found it helpful to organize similar things into groups. For instance, there are many kinds of chairs, but you can still group them as human-made structures that a person sits on. The process of grouping things according to the characteristics they share is called **classification**.

Libraries, for example, have classification systems to keep track of their books. Imagine going to a library where the books had no titles and were shelved any old way. To find a specific book, you would have to look at every book on every shelf. Luckily, books are given titles, and libraries organize them according to characteristics they share.

Libraries have different sections for cookbooks, science fiction, and poetry. If you are looking for poetry, you know to go directly to that section.

Just as a library is full of books, Earth is full of an extraordinary abundance and variety of organisms (living things). More than two million different kinds of organisms have been identified so far. More are found all the time. Scientists name and classify all of these organisms to keep track of them.

After an earthquake in California, the Honnold/ Mudd Library's books became very disorganized.

Background image: In its lakes, forests, and other habitats, Earth teems with life.

Libraries have detailed filing systems to organize their books.

Classifying Life

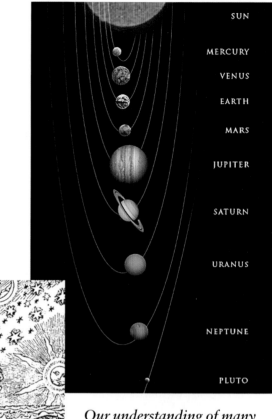

People group living things differently, according to their own particular needs and interests. For some people, the most important characteristic of a living thing is its usefulness. At one time, all animals were grouped as useful, harmful, or unnecessary, and all plants as producing fruits, vegetables, fibers, or wood. Even today, farmers classify farm animals and plants according to their use: cows for milking and cows for beef, horses for working and horses for riding, grains to feed livestock and grains to feed people.

As our understanding of Earth has changed, so have our ideas about how to classify organisms. Some ancient peoples grouped all known objects into one of three categories: mineral (non-living things), vegetable (plants), or animal (animals).

Our understanding of many things has changed over time. People used to think Earth was flat, now we know that Earth is a round planet that orbits around the sun.

Then, more than 2,000 years ago, the Greek scientist Aristotle divided plants and animals into three categories each. He divided plants into herbs, shrubs, or trees. He grouped animals according to where they lived: on land, in water, or in the air. Aristotle also recognized that both plants and animals ranged from simple to complex beings.

SUN
MERCURY
VENUS
EARTH
MARS
JUPITER
SATURN
URANUS
NEPTUNE
PLUTO

The Greek scientist Aristotle classified plants as herbs (top), shrubs (middle), or trees (bottom). He classified animals by where they lived: land (top), water (middle), or air (bottom).

Aristotle

Herb

Land animal

Shrub

Water animal

Tree

Air animal

Scientists still use the classification and naming system that Carolus Linnaeus created in the 1700s.

In the 1700s, Carolus Linnaeus, a Swedish biologist, developed a universal system to name and classify organisms. He grouped them according to their physical characteristics. In other words, he classified them by what they looked like. Linnaeus's system worked so well that it became the basis for how all scientists name, classify, and communicate about living things. We call the process of classifying living things **taxonomy.**

9

Common Names and Scientific Names

Linnaeus classified more than 11,000 organisms during his lifetime! He called similar organisms **species,** the Latin word meaning "appearance" or "kind." Organisms in a species shared the same characteristics and could also reproduce to make an offspring (baby) of the same species.

He also gave each species a unique name that all people could use no matter what language they spoke.

While a dog has many common names around the world, its scientific name is always Canis familiarus.

For example, a "dog" in England is a "perro" in Argentina, and a "hund" in Germany. Some scientists attempted to translate these common names for organisms into one language but found it very difficult. Instead, Linnaeus decided to give each species a brand-new, two-part name in Latin or Greek that would be its official scientific name.

The first part of a scientific name stands for an organism's **genus.** A genus is a group of related species. The second part identifies the actual species that an organism belongs to. For example, a *Felis canadensis* is a Canadian lynx and a *Felis domesticus* is a house cat. Both animals share the same first name because they are

An elephant (Loxindonta africana) *can only reproduce with another elephant. The baby will also be an elephant.*

The Canadian lynx, Felis canadensis, (left) is in the same genus as the domestic cat, Felis domesticus (right).

grouped in the genus *Felis*, meaning catlike animals. But they are different enough to be separated into two species: *canadensis* (which means "from Canada") and *domesticus* (which means "home").

The Icelandic falcon, Falco islandus, *was first identified in Iceland.*

Linnaeus's system of two-word naming, known as **binomial nomenclature**, is still used today when naming new species. Most names are created as a memory tool. Some species are named after a person (*Amanita caesarea* is Caesar's mushroom), some after the place they were first found (*Falco islandus* for the Icelandic falcon), but most names use a descriptive word. For example, the black rhinoceros, *Diceros bicornis*, has two horns and the word "bicornis" means "two horns" in Latin. In every-day conversation, people use common names— falcon, mushroom, rhinoceros, and so on. But when scientists discuss specific organisms, they use their scientific names.

Caesar's mushroom, Amanita caesarea, *was named for Julius Caesar, a famous Roman emperor.*

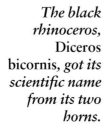

The black rhinoceros, Diceros bicornis, *got its scientific name from its two horns.*

Taxonomy

For Linnaeus, giving names to species was like giving titles to books. He then went on to develop a filing system that grouped species together according to their similarities, the way librarians create sections in a library.

Linnaeus divided all life into two kingdoms: plants and animals. Within each kingdom, certain species share more characteristics with one another than they do with other organisms.

Although all three are animals, a dog (middle) is more similar to a house cat (bottom) than to a jellyfish (top).

So Linnaeus divided each kingdom into smaller groups, called phyla (singular: phylum) for animals and divisions for plants. Again, within each phylum or division, certain groups of species were more alike than others. These groups were sorted into classes of similar organisms. Classes were further divided into orders, orders into families, and families into genera (singular: genus). Each genus, which is the first part of an organism's scientific name, contained groups of the most similar organisms—the species.

Flowering plants, such as a torch ginger (top) and a pink azalea (middle), are more closely related to each other than they are to nonflowering plants such as this interrupted fern (bottom).

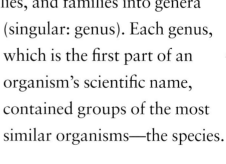

In all, Linnaeus created seven levels, or categories, of classification. The more levels two organisms share, the more similar they are. For example, a jellyfish is an animal and a rose is a plant. They do not share any levels of classification and are not at all alike. A cat and a dog, on the other hand, share the same kingdom, phylum, and class, but are in different orders, families, genera, and species. They are somewhat similar. A Canadian lynx and a house cat share the same kingdom, phylum, class, order, family, and genus. They are much more similar than a cat is to a dog.

Animal Kingdom

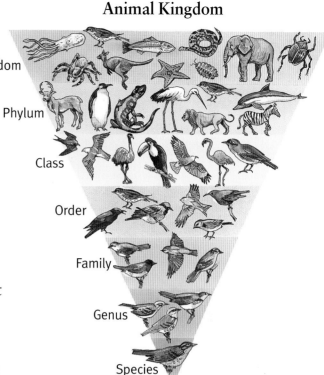

Kingdom

Phylum

Class

Order

Family

Genus

Species

Plant Kingdom

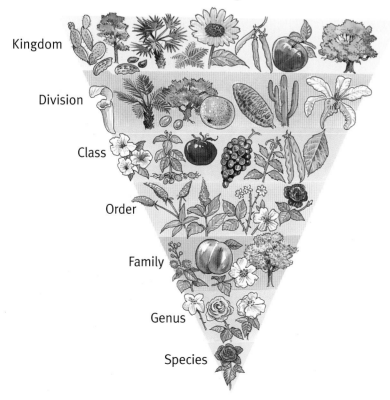

Kingdom

Division

Class

Order

Family

Genus

Species

Two organisms, the blackburnian warbler (Dendroica fusca) *and the moss rose* (Rosa gallica), *are shown classified within Linnaeus's seven levels of classification. As the illustration narrows from kingdom to species, you can see how each level has fewer and fewer kinds of organisms.*

The Microscope: A Tool for Scientists

The **microscope** is an important tool for biologists, scientists who study life. Microscopes greatly magnify the size of an object. That is, they make it look much bigger than it really is. By using microscopes, biologists have observed many details about the structure of all living things. This knowledge has helped scientists refine and expand upon Linnaeus's classification system.

Early microscopes revealed **microorganisms**, tiny living things that people never knew existed before, because they were too small to see with just your eyes.

The microscope Anton van Leeuwenhoek used in the late 1600s to observe microscopic creatures could magnify an image up to 200 times its normal size.

Today, scientists and students alike use compound microscopes.

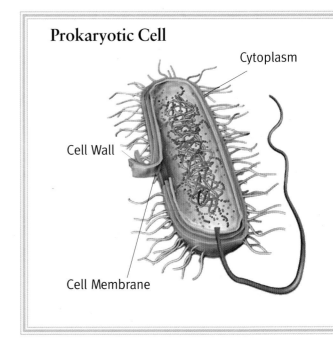

Prokaryotic Cell

Cytoplasm

Cell Wall

Cell Membrane

Microscopes also enabled biologists to see that all living things are made up of tiny living building blocks called **cells.** Cells give a body structure and carry out the activities it needs to survive. All cells are made of a jellylike substance, called **cytoplasm,** which holds the materials and chemicals of the cell. A **cell membrane** surrounds the cytoplasm, holding a cell together. Most microorganisms are made of a single cell; larger organisms are made of many cells.

Using his microscope in the 1800s, Louis Pasteur studied many disease-causing microorganisms.

There are two basic kinds of cells: prokaryotic *and* eukaryotic. *Every organism is made up of one kind or the other.*

Prokaryotic cells are simpler and much smaller than eukaryotic cells. Most have a cell wall, *but they lack enclosed organelles. Instead, all their materials and chemicals sit directly in their cytoplasm.*

Eukaryotic cells have a number of organelles ("little organs") in their cytoplasm. Organelles are the "machinery" that carry out a cell's activities. The most important organelle is the nucleus. *Many eukaryotic cells also have a rigid* cell wall. *Animal cells do not have cell walls.*

Animal Eukaryotic Cell

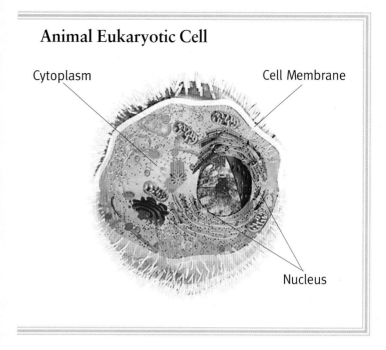

Cytoplasm

Cell Membrane

Nucleus

Today's most powerful microscopes, called **electron microscopes**, make objects appear up to one million times larger than normal! Invented in the 1930s, electron microscopes enabled biologists to study the details *inside* cells. They observed how the structure and behavior of plant and animal cells were quite different from each other. In addition, they discovered that certain organisms were not plants or animals at all.

To account for these nonplant, nonanimal organisms, biologists added new categories to taxonomy. For example, mushrooms used to be classified as plants.

Here at Columbia University's Lamont-Doherty Earth Observatory, scientist Dee Berger can magnify the image of an object more than one million times using an electron microscope.

Now they are a part of the Kingdom Fungi, which also includes molds and yeasts.

Life's Family Tree

Linnaeus used classification as an organizing tool to keep track of Earth's different organisms. Today, scientists use classification to represent how organisms are related to each other—life's family tree. **Genetics** is a branch of science that studies these relationships between organisms.

In genetics, scientists study **genes**, the chemical directions for making an organism. Genes are found in every cell of every organism. When organisms reproduce, they pass on their genes to their offspring. Thus, an offspring's genes—the directions to make its body—are a combination of the genes of its parents.

Scientists compare the genes of different organisms to learn how they are related. In general, the more similar the genes of two organisms are, the more closely the organisms are related. Siblings with the same parents, for example puppies from the same litter, are closely related and have nearly identical genes. Organisms that share a set of grandparents are less closely related. They have slightly different genes. A sunflower and a worm are not at all closely related and have very different genes. Once the genetic

Phylogenic Tree

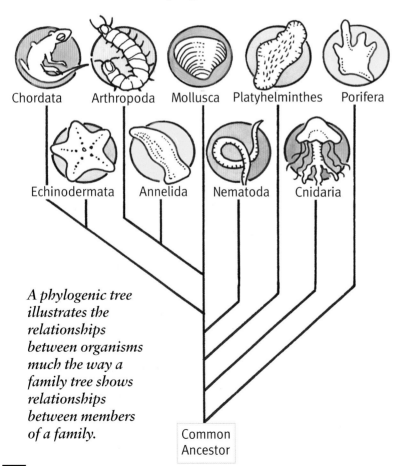

A phylogenic tree illustrates the relationships between organisms much the way a family tree shows relationships between members of a family.

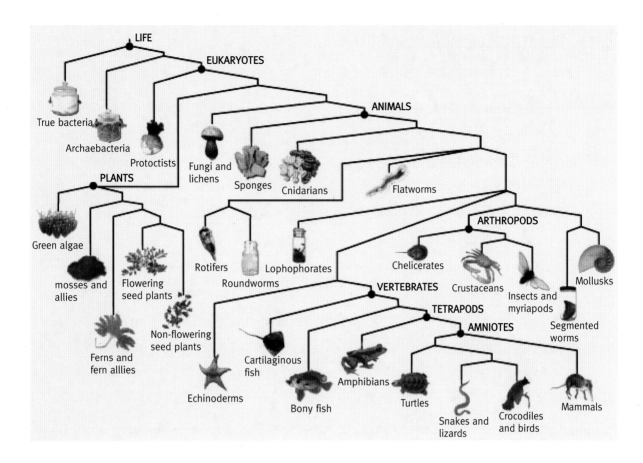

The following labels appear on the life tree diagram:

LIFE
EUKARYOTES
ANIMALS
True bacteria
Archaebacteria
Protoctists
Fungi and lichens
Sponges
Cnidarians
Flatworms
PLANTS
ARTHROPODS
Green algae
Rotifers
Lophophorates
Chelicerates
Mollusks
mosses and allies
Flowering seed plants
Roundworms
VERTEBRATES
Crustaceans
Insects and myriapods
TETRAPODS
Segmented worms
Non-flowering seed plants
AMNIOTES
Ferns and fern alllies
Cartilaginous fish
Amphibians
Turtles
Mammals
Echinoderms
Bony fish
Snakes and lizards
Crocodiles and birds

A life tree shows the relationships of organisms throughout Earth's history. Begin at the top left, where it says "LIFE." As you move to the right, each new branch indicates the development of a new kind of organism. The pictures on each branch illustrate life today.

relationships between organisms are understood, scientists can draw a phylogenic tree ("family tree") that shows the relationships.

Scientists can also extract genes from **fossils,** the preserved remains of ancient organisms. Comparing the genes from fossils to those from animals living today suggests that modern species are distantly related to ancient organisms.

Though Linnaeus knew nothing about genetics when developing taxonomy, his classification system does a good job of representing the relationships between organisms. He grouped organisms according to similar characteristics, and for the most part, organisms with similar genes also have similar characteristics.

In a few cases, however, having similar characteristics does not mean that organisms are closely related. For example, birds and insects both have wings. But bird genes are quite different from insect genes. Therefore, these animals are not at all closely related.

Six Kingdoms of Life

Today organisms are placed into kingdoms based on the general characteristics they share and their degree of relatedness with other members of that kingdom. Not all organisms fit neatly into only one kingdom, however. Because of this, scientists disagree about how many kingdoms there should be and how some organisms should be classified. This book follows a system in which life is organized into six kingdoms: Kingdom Archaebacteria, Kingdom Eubacteria, Kingdom Protista, Kingdom Fungi, Kingdom Planta, and Kingdom Animalia.

Archaebacteria are simple organisms made up of a single **prokaryotic** cell. They live in very extreme environments, such as deep-sea vents, where there is no oxygen. "Archae" means "ancient," and scientists think that archaebacteria were among the first organisms.

Eubacteria include all other single-celled prokaryotic organisms. They are the "true" bacteria and can be found everywhere on Earth. Some help to break down food and dead organisms into useful nutrients. Others can be harmful and cause disease.

Protists, including algae, protozoa, and slime molds, are the smallest organisms made from **eukaryotic** cells. Most are single-celled. They live wherever it is wet. Evidence suggests that protists evolved from bacteria. Some species, in turn, evolved into animals, plants, and fungi.

Fungi, including mushrooms, molds, and yeasts, are eukaryotic organisms. Their cells have walls. They don't eat the way animals do, but absorb nutrients from plants and animals – dead and alive. They can grow very quickly and are essential to the health of the natural world.

Plants, including trees, grasses, and shrubs, are multicelled eukaryotic organisms. Most live on land, but evidence suggests that they evolved from algae. Their cells have walls and contain chlorophyll, a substance that makes them green. Chlorophyll helps plants make their own food through a chemical reaction called photosynthesis.

Animals, including mammals, insects, and fish, are multicelled eukaryotic organisms. Their cells have membranes but lack cell walls. They have to eat plants and other animals for food. Animals are the most mobile organisms. Most can slither, crawl, swim, walk, run, climb, or even fly.

*Background image: A black rhinoceros (*Diceros bicorni*) grazes in the grasslands of the Ngorongoro Crater, Tanzania.*

The first two kingdoms, Archaebacteria and Eubacteria, consist of the world's tiniest organisms, bacteria. Made of a single prokaryotic cell, they are so small that you can only see them with a microscope. Some grow together into large, visible colonies, but you still cannot make out the individuals without a microscope. Even under a simple light microscope, bacteria look like small dots. It takes a powerful electron microscope to actually see their structure and behavior. Most bacteria are rod shaped (*bacillus*), round (*coccus*), or spiral (*spirillum*). Although tiny and simple, bacteria dramatically affect our lives and have played a major role in the history of life on Earth. They are the most successful and abundant forms of life on Earth, and they have been since life on Earth began. For more than half Earth's history, bacteria were the only living organisms.

Shigella *bacteria (top) live in the intestines of animals.* Streptococcus *bacteria (middle) cause throat infections ("strep throat").* Spiral Borrelia burgdorferi *bacteria (bottom) cause Lyme disease.*

Kingdom Archaebacteria

When Earth was forming, there was no oxygen. Therefore, early bacteria had to survive without it. Kingdom Archaebacteria includes both ancient bacteria and present day bacteria that live without oxygen.

Archaebacteria are sometimes called "extremeophiles"—lovers of extreme environments ("phile" means "to love.") They are often studied according to the extreme environments in which they live.

Archaebacteria can be found in deep sea vents called black smokers.

Thermophiles are the heat lovers. As you might imagine, they live in hot environments, such as hot springs. Some, the hyperthermophiles, thrive in extremely hot conditions. In Yellowstone, Wyoming, archaebacteria can survive in springs so hot the water is actually boiling!

Great Salt Lake in Utah is saltier than the ocean. Halophile bacteria thrive here.

Thermophile bacteria love hot environments without oxygen.

Halophiles are the salt lovers (halite is the mineral name for salt.) They can survive only in water with a high concentration of salt—even saltier than the ocean. These bacteria are found in the Great Salt Lake, Utah, and the Dead Sea in the Middle East.

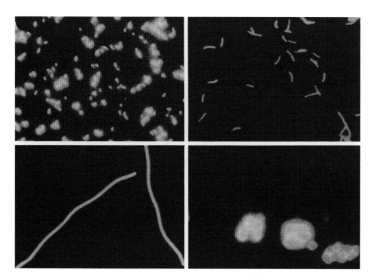

Methanogens produce methane gas. Some live in animals' intestines and help break down food into usable nutrients. Others live deep in the ocean near vents from underwater volcanoes.

Methanogen bacteria come in many different shapes and sizes.

Kingdom Eubacteria

All other bacteria—the "true" bacteria—are grouped in the Kingdom Eubacteria. Many are helpful to other organisms, but some cause diseases. Eubacteria are often classified according to how they obtain nutrients for energy. In each name, "troph" means "nourishment."

Autotrophs ("self nourishment") make their own food. **Photo-autotrophs** ("self nourishment from sunlight") make their food from sunlight. They contain **chlorophyll**, a green substance that uses sunlight to combine minerals, water, and carbon dioxide to form sugar, the most basic kind of food. This chemical reaction is called **photosynthesis** (see page 32 for more on photosynthesis).

Cyanobacteria are photoautotrophs. They make their own food using sunlight.

Chemo-autotrophs ("self nourishment from chemicals") make their food from chemicals containing sulfur, iron, or nitrogen. For example, nitrogen-fixing bacteria help take nitrogen from the soil and change it into a form that is usable by other organisms. Some actually live inside the roots of plants as nitrogen-fixing "machines."

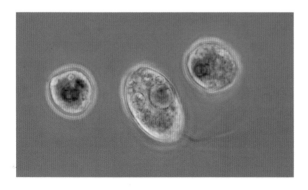

The chemo-autotroph Rhizobium leguminosarium *processes nitrogen in the roots of white clover plants.*

Heterotrophs ("other nourishment") cannot make their own food. Instead, they absorb nutrients from other organisms. Some, the decomposers, break down the bodies of dead organisms. Dead bodies contain a lot of nutrients, and these bacteria recycle the nutrients back into the environment to be used again. Others, the parasites, feed off living organisms. Often parasites make the host organism sick.

These heterotrophs were found in the cold water of a lake in winter.

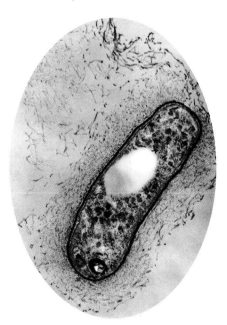

People make models of viruses to better understand whether or not they should be considered living things.

Viruses: *On the border of living and non-living*

Scientists debate whether or not viruses are alive at all. This affects whether they should be classified in one of the kingdoms of life. Viruses are tiny, but they are not bacteria. Their bodies are not made of cells, but they do contain materials found in cells. They can reproduce, but only if they use the cell of another organism. Although viruses may not be alive, they affect living things by causing diseases. That is why many biologists, people who study living things, also study viruses.

Kingdom Protista

Protists thrive in wet environments. Most are single-celled, but some, such as seaweed, can grow quite large. They are the most abundant eukaryotic organisms in oceans and lakes. Some also live inside the moist bodies of animals and plants.

Protists are often grouped according to whether they are plantlike, animal-like, or funguslike. In fact, they were placed in the plant and animal kingdoms until scientists decided that their characteristics did not quite match those kingdoms. Kingdom Protista is a catch-all for eukaryotic organisms that do not fit into the other kingdoms.

Animallike Protists

Animallike protists, called **protozoa**, cannot make their own food. Instead they take in food as animals do. They are the most mobile protists and are often classified according to how they move.

Background image: The bodies of amoebas and most protists are transparent. Under a microscope, you can see their organelles and cytoplasm.

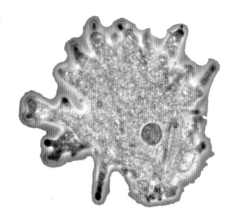

An amoeba is a protozoan that changes its body shape as it moves.

Flagellates look like a cell with tails. They move by flapping their **flagella,** whiplike structures that wag back and forth. Many flagellates can be parasitic.

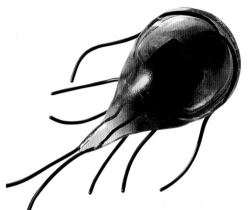

Giardia lamblia *is a flagellate found in fresh water that causes illness in humans. It has many flagella to help it move.*

Amoebas resemble jellylike blobs and move by changing shape. They push their cell membranes in the direction they want to go and let the materials inside the cell ooze into the new space. They move very slowly— they can take days just to move an inch or two. They feed by encircling a food particle and drawing it into their cell through the membrane.

Ciliates move by fluttering their short hairlike appendages called **cilia.** Cilia coordinate to propel the cell in a corkscrewlike movement. A paramecium, the most complex of all protozoa, is a ciliate with specialized structures including a mouth.

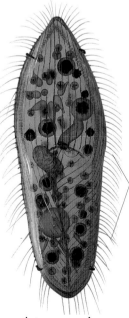

Cilia

A paramecium looks hairy because of its many cilia.

Sporozoa are tiny parasitic protozoa that only live in the cells of other organisms. They have no cilia or flagella, and instead rely on their host for movement. *Plasmodium* is a sporozoan that causes malaria.

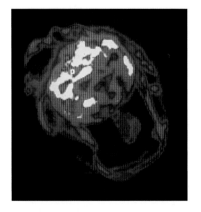

Plasmodium falciparum *is a sporozoan.*

Plantlike Protists

Algae are the plantlike protists. If you've ever seen pond scum, you've seen algae. If you like sushi, you've eaten a different kind of algae. Algae actually exist in a number of colors including brown, red, and green. Like plants and some bacteria, they make their own food through photosynthesis (see page 32). Algae produce most of the oxygen we breathe.

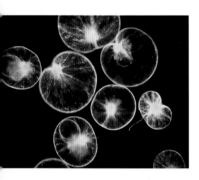

Sea sparkles (Noctiluca scintillans) are a kind of dinoflagellate that give off light, making the ocean appear to "sparkle" at night.

Single-celled algae, such as **dinoflagellates** and **diatoms**, are phytoplankton—plantlike organisms that float in water. Filter-feeding animals depend on plankton for food. Individual phytoplankton are not easily visible with the naked eye. In large

colonies, however, dinoflagellates can give ocean water a reddish tint and cause what are known as "red tides."

Seaweeds, such as *Ulva*, or sea lettuce, are large multicelled algae. One of the most well known is *Porphyra*, a red seaweed used to wrap sushi (fresh, raw fish). In Japanese food dishes it is called "nori."

Sea lettuce (Ulva lactuca)

The largest and most complex algae are the brown algae, including sea palms (*Postelsia*) and kelp. Kelp grow into vast underwater forests. They anchor to the seafloor and grow up toward the light. They have been measured up to 70 meters in height.

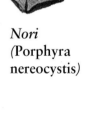

Nori (Porphyra nereocystis)

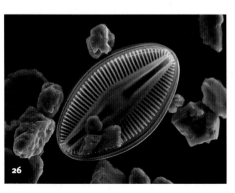

The cell walls of a diatom can be quite intricate.

Sea palm (Postelsia palmaeformis)

Funguslike Protists

Slime molds, water molds, and downy mildews all look and act like fungi, but their cell structure and life cycles are more closely related to those of amoebas.

Slime molds are usually bright yellow or orange. They are jellylike and found in moist environments. They creep slowly along, feeding on bacteria and bits of dead and decaying organisms.

*Eggyolk slime (*Fuligo septica*) grows on a stick.*

Water molds also help to decompose dead insects, fish, and other animals. They usually grow as cottony masses on dead algae and animals in fresh water. Some grow on living organisms as parasites.

Downy mildew live on land plants. They can ruin food crops. One caused the Irish potato famine in the 1840s, which killed most of the potato crop in Ireland, and caused many people to starve.

These potatoes have been infected with a downy mildew.

This goldfish looks furry because a water mold is growing on it.

Kingdom Fungi

The fruiting body of a mushroom grows above ground.

Fungi can make food rot, your sneakers smell, and your toes itch. But they also help to make bread and cheese and can be quite tasty. These organisms cannot move around the way animals do, and for a long time they were grouped with plants, but they cannot make their own food, either. Over time, scientists have agreed that these organisms should be classified as Kingdom Fungi.

Fungi take in nutrients, but they do not eat food the way animals do. Instead a fungus breaks down food outside its body. Fungi grow on the outside of their food and break it down using strong chemicals, called **enzymes**. Once the food is broken down, fungi absorb the nutrients through their cell walls.

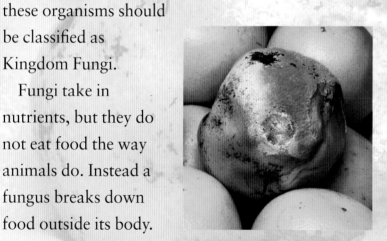

A moldy grapefruit can become white and furry.

Fungi include mushrooms, cup fungi, and molds. Most live off organisms that are dead. They are decomposers, like some bacteria. They break down and recycle nutrients back into the water and soil.

Mushrooms have been a popular food for thousands of years. The mushroom cap, the part we eat, is the "fruiting body" of the fungus. Most of the organism actually lives underground and can grow quite large. If you see clumps of mushrooms in different places in a park, they might all be from one giant individual fungus.

On the underside of the cap are slitlike openings called gills that produce special reproductive cells called spores. Spores are carried by the wind and grow into mushrooms in a new location.

Molds grow on food, turning it brown, green, white, or black depending on the type of mold. They develop microscopic fruiting bodies that look like tiny lollipops. The "lollipop" is a case that bursts open releasing tiny cells, called spores, into the air that land on other food. Molds grow faster in moist, warm conditions. That is why food keeps better if you store it in a refrigerator or freezer.

Histoplasma *fungus can cause a mild disease in humans and animals.*

Piptoporus betulinus *is a fungus that grows on birch trees.*

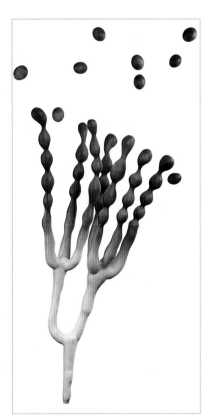

Penicillium *mold is used to make the antibiotic medicine called penicillin.*

Lichens are a combination of fungi and algae. They grow on rocks, plants, and animals.

Kingdom Planta

When you walk through a park, trees tower above you, grass cushions your feet, and moss clings to rocks. You are surrounded by plants. In fact, you owe your life to them. Your morning cereal is made from grains, your juice squeezed from fruit. The meat you eat comes from animals that ate plants. Plants provide much of the oxygen in the very air you breathe. They are essential to the survival of most of Earth's organisms.

Like many bacteria and protists, plant cells contain chlorophyll to help them make food through photosynthesis. Chlorophyll is the chemical that makes plants look green.

Screw pine (Pandanus utilis) *has sword-shaped leaves that grow in a spiral.*

All plants are multicellular. Plants have two main body types: **vascular** and **nonvascular**. Vascular plants have tubelike structures that transport water and other materials from one part of the plant to another. Nonvascular plants do not have these structures. Instead they grow near the ground, so their cells can get nutrients and water directly from the soil.

Background image: A ripe stalk of Indian corn (Zea mays).

Nonvascular plants

Nonvascular plants reproduce by sending spores into the air. Spores drift to a new location, where they land and create a new plant. They can also send underground extensions, called runners, to an unoccupied patch of soil. From the runner, a new plant grows up out of the ground.

This liverwort (Adelanthus decipiens) *looks glossy green when wet, and almost black when dry.*

Moss are plants that often grows on other plants, including trees.

Liverworts and **hornworts** are two other nonvascular plants. "Wort" means herb. A long time ago, people thought that liverworts could cure liver diseases. Hornworts grow in a horn shape. Like moss, both liverworts and hornworts use rhizoids to cling to the soil.

Mosses are the most common nonvascular plants. They grow in large mats on rocks, trees, and forest floors and in wetlands. They prefer damp, moist environments and anchor themselves into the soil with rootlike threads called **rhizoids**. A mat of moss is actually a colony of many individual plants.

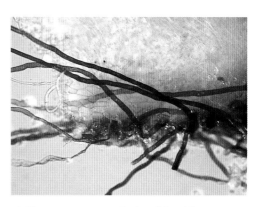

A liverwort extends its rhizoids to cling to the soil.

Vascular Plants

Trees, grasses, ferns, and vines—most of the plants on Earth—are vascular plants. As ancient algae left the oceans to live on land, they evolved rigid cell walls to support their bodies out of the water. On land, the water and minerals needed for photosynthesis are found in the soil. So these plants evolved a system of tubes through which substances from the soil could be transported through their bodies. These tubes allowed vascular plants to grow up, away from the soil.

All vascular plants have a similar set of structures. **Roots** extend below ground. They absorb water and minerals from the soil and serve as an anchor. **Shoots**, including **stems** and **leaves**, grow above ground. They contain chlorophyll and carry out photosynthesis. A two-way piping system branches through the entire plant. **Xylem** is made of the walls of cells that fuse to create a set of hollow tubes running from the roots to the shoots. It is through this pathway that water and nutrients are transported from the soil to the photosynthesizing cells.

Photosynthesis

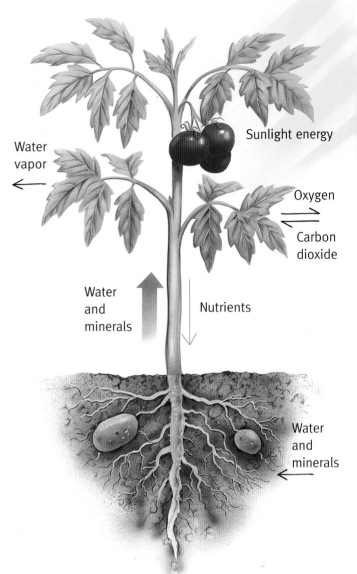

Sunlight energy

Water vapor

Oxygen

Carbon dioxide

Water and minerals

Nutrients

Water and minerals

In photosynthesis, plants, algae, and some bacteria make food from sunlight, water, and carbon dioxide. This diagram shows photosynthesis in vascular plants. The roots draw minerals and water from the soil and send them up the stem to the leaves. The leaves draw carbon dioxide from the air. In the plant's cells, a substance called chlorophyll helps converts the carbon dioxide and water into food with the help of sunlight. The food is either used right away or stored in the plant's fruit and roots for later use.

Phloem, made of living tissues, moves the food made in the shoots throughout the plant. The xylem and phloem are the reason these plants can grow so tall.

Trees are the largest vascular plants. When someone cuts down a tree, you can tell its age by counting the growth rings in its trunk, the tree's stem. Growth rings are actually layers of xylem, the woody material inside a tree. The outer protective layer on a tree, called bark, is the phloem. The thin layer between the xylem and phloem in a tree trunk is called **cambium**. The cambium layer generates the new xylem and phloem layers as a tree grows.

Paperbark tree (Melaleuca quinquervia)

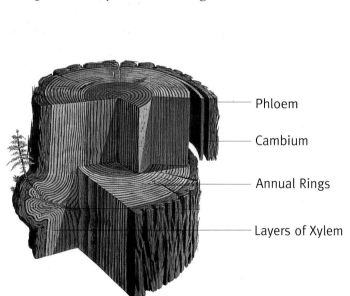

— Phloem

— Cambium

— Annual Rings

— Layers of Xylem

Notice the growth rings inside the trunk of this west coast redwood tree (Sequoia sempervirens).

Ferns are vascular plants with leaves that look like large feathers. They reproduce using spores, which grow in cases on the underside of a fern's leaves. Ferns were once the dominant plant on Earth and grew quite large in vast forests and swamps. These ancient forests grew so fast that the forest floor became thickly layered with plant debris. These layers were eventually buried deep in the ground and over millions of years became the coal we use today.

Background image: Old World climbing ferns (Lygodium microphyllum)

Flowering fern (Osmunda regalis)

Coal made from ancient ferns

Fossil fern

Many vascular plants reproduce using **seeds**. A seed is a capsule that protects a developing plant inside a seed wall. The seed also contains a supply of food for the developing plant to use until it can grow on its own.

Gymnosperms are seed-producing plants that have no flowers. Their seeds often grow inside hard woody cases called cones. Conifers, such as pines, spruce, and fir trees, are the most well known gymnosperms. Most have needle-shaped or scalelike leaves. These

The jack pine has a J-shaped cone. The Scots pine has an egg-shaped cone. The largest conifers, the redwoods, have some of the smallest and some of the largest cones.

Most conifers grow well in cooler climates. The farther from the equator you go, the more conifers you see. The trees in Alaskan forests are almost all conifers.

Pine cones grow on the tips of branches (1). When a pine cone opens (2), the seeds fall to the ground. A conifer's needles are its leaves (3). Almost all the trees in Alaskan forests are conifers (4).

trees have earned the nickname "evergreen" because they do not lose their leaves in winter the way many other trees do. Conifers come in all shapes and sizes, and their cones are just as varied. You can identify a gymnosperm just by looking at its cone.

The ginkgo tree is a gymnosperm but not a conifer. Its leaves are fan-shaped and they fall off the tree seasonally. Its seeds give off a rotten odor but are often collected for food and tea.

Ginkgo leaf
(Ginkgo bioloba)

Angiosperms are seed-producing plants that have flowers and fruits. They are the most abundant plants on Earth. You'll find angiosperms blooming not only in lush forests and gardens, but also on the arctic tundra, in the desert, and in the cracks of city sidewalks. Not all flowers have bright colors like orchids and roses. Grasses and nut trees are angiosperms, too.

The flower of a passion fruit (**Passiflora edulis**).

Pistil

Stamen

Petal

The main purpose of a flower is reproduction. An angiosperm is ready to reproduce if it is in bloom. When a flower opens its petals, it reveals the plant's reproductive structures, the **stamen** and **pistils**, at its center. The stamen produces a sticky powder called **pollen**, which is the substance that fertilizes a plant's seeds. Pistils are the tubelike tops of the plant's **ovaries**, the structures in which seeds develop. Pistils catch pollen and help it to enter the ovaries.

Grass (**Melica transsiranica**)

A flower's color and scent attract certain birds, insects, and bats to the plant. These animals, called **pollinators**, help angiosperms reproduce by transporting pollen from one flower to the pistils of another. Pollen sticks to their bodies as they feed on **nectar**, the sweet sugar-water made by flowers. Then, as they move from plant to plant, the pollen on their bodies rubs off on the pistils of other flowers.

Once an angiosperm is fertilized, the ovaries turn into a fruit that protects the seeds while they develop. The fruit also helps to transport the seeds to a place with enough soil, water, and sunlight to **germinate**, or grow into a new plant. Some fruits are tiny and light enough to be dispersed by the wind. Larger, fleshy fruits taste sweet and are eaten by animals. The fruit can be digested, but the seeds cannot. So the animals serve as transportation for the seeds. The seeds pass out of the animals and find a new place to germinate.

Fruit grows on a papaya tree (Carica papaya).

Germination (below) is the process by which a new plant forms from a seed into a seedling, or baby plant. A seed germinates when water enters the seed coat, causing it to swell. Roots break out of the seed in search of water and minerals in the soil. A tiny shoot grows out of the seed. Eventually, leaves sprout from the shoot, and the plant begins to make its food through photosynthesis.

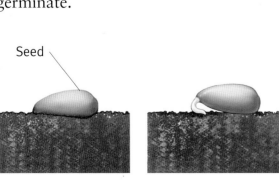

Seed

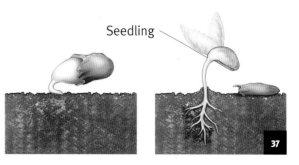

Seedling

Kingdom Animalia

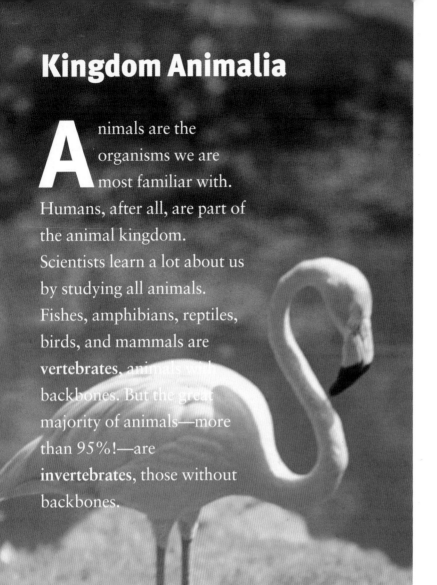

Animals are the organisms we are most familiar with. Humans, after all, are part of the animal kingdom. Scientists learn a lot about us by studying all animals. Fishes, amphibians, reptiles, birds, and mammals are **vertebrates**, animals with backbones. But the great majority of animals—more than 95%!—are **invertebrates**, those without backbones.

Invertebrates

Porifera are simple aquatic invertebrates also known as sponges. They filter water through the pores (holes) in their bodies. For the most part, they stay anchored to one spot on the ocean floor. They were once mistaken for plants.

American flamingo (Phoenicopterus ruber)

Sponges, such as this vase sponge, are often named for their appearance.

Sea anemones were once thought of as plants. Their tentacles look like blooming flowers.

Cnidaria, including corals, sea anemones, and jellyfish, feed with long tentacles that sting and stun prey. The word "cnidaria" means "stinging nettles." Adult jellyfish spend most of their lives floating in oceans. Corals and sea anemones usually stay anchored to a rock or reef, and were once mistaken for plants. They are now called Anthozoa ("flowering animals") because when they extend their tentacles, they look like blooming flowers.

Platyhelminthes, **nematodes**, and **annelids** are some of the many kinds of slithering, soft-bodied animals known as worms. Platyhelminthes, or flatworms, have the simplest body structures. Most are small and feed on tiny animals or dead organisms. Others, such as tapeworms, are parasitic. They live in the intestines of animals and eat the food the animals digest.

Notice the segments on these two earthworms.

Segment

Nematoda, or roundworms, have cylindrical bodies that taper off at each end. They thrive in moist environments—water, wet soil, and the tissues of plants and animals. Annelida, or segmented worms, have more complex bodies than other worms, including a network of nerves and organ systems for digestion and circulation. Among annelids, earthworms have five hearts, and leeches use suckers to hold onto their prey while they feed on its blood.

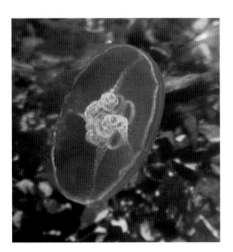

The body of a moon jelly (Aurelia aurita) is so clear that you can see its insides.

Mollusks include clams, snails, and octopuses. While these animals look very different from one another, they share three characteristics: a soft main body containing the organs, a protective layer of skin that can turn into a shell, and a foot. Most mollusks grow a hard shell, or pair of shells, to hide inside. Clams and oysters have two shells connected by a hinge that opens and shuts. Snails grow a spiral-shaped shell which they carry on their backs. The octopus has lost the ability to make a shell. In addition, its muscular foot has adapted into eight appendages, which are well-suited for movement. With its large brain, an octopus is one of the most intelligent of all invertebrate animals.

Arthropods are a huge group, including spiders, insects, millipedes, centipedes, and crabs. There are more varieties of arthropods than any other kind of animal. Each arthropod has a segmented body, jointed legs, and a hard protective covering called an exoskeleton ("skeleton on the outside").

This museum diorama recreates the habitat of octopuses and squid.

The fungus beetle feeds on fungus.

A glorious beetle (Plusiotis gloriosa) has distinct metallic markings on its iridescent body.

Sea cucumbers are some of the most abundant animals in the ocean.

Millipedes have long bodies with many segments and legs. Spiders have two segments and eight legs. In crustaceans, one pair of legs is adapted into claws for defense and grabbing prey. Most insects have one or two pairs of wings. Insects are the most abundant kind of animal on Earth.

Echinoderms, including sea stars, sea cucumbers, and sea urchins, have hard, prickly, often spiny outer layers. The main body is a central disk from which appendages grow—five arms with most echinoderms, and as many as 20 with some sea stars.

Water is pumped through the many tube feet of echinoderms, enabling them to move. The feet also act as suction cups for attaching to rocks and other surfaces.

A sea star lives on the ocean floor.

Vertebrates

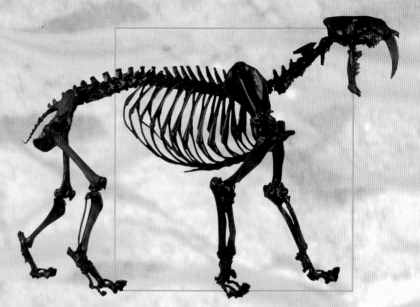

The phylum Chordata includes animals from sea squirts and fish through mammals. These animals all share a flexible rod, called the notochord, that supports the body. Vertebrates make up a large part of the chordates.

Vertebrate animals have well-developed sense organs with a brain in the front, or head end. All have vertebrae (backbones) that surround the spinal cord and a skull that protects the brain.

A skeleton of the saber tooth cat (Smilodon populator) *clearly shows its bones.*

Most have two pairs of appendages (fins, wings, legs, or arms). Their skeletons grow as they grow.

Fish are the most abundant vertebrates and are thought to have been the first animals to develop vertebrae. They live in water—oceans, lakes, or streams. Fish breathe by taking in oxygen from water through their gills. Most will suffocate if they are out of the water for very long. Fish swim using a pair of fins, a strong tail, and a streamlined body covered with scales.

Guppies (Poecilia reticulata) *make good pets because they are peaceful, lively, and hardy.*

Amphibians are vertebrates that need to live in or near water. If you've ever held a frog or salamander, you know how damp its skin is. Adult amphibians have simple lungs that do not take in much oxygen, so they also breathe through their skin. In order to do this, their skin has to be moist, so they never go too far from water. The word "amphibian" means "two lives;" these animals can live in both land and water. Amphibian bodies go through a

*Northern red salamander (*Pseudotrion ruber ruber)

*Mexican tree frog (*Smilisca baudinii)

*California newt (*Taricha torosa)

metamorphosis, or change, as they grow and develop. For instance, frogs begin life as tiny tadpoles with gills to breathe oxygen in water and a tail for swimming. Then they grow legs, lose their tails, and become adults that breathe oxygen from air. Scientists believe that salamanders and frogs evolved from fishes, whose fins adapted into legs for walking on land. Vertebrates belong to a larger group called chordates, which include sea squirts and turnicates.

Reptiles, including snakes, lizards, crocodiles, and turtles, all breathe air. Some live on land and some in water.

A spotted turtle (Clemys guttata) *suns itself on a rock.*

Although diverse, they are thought to have evolved from similar ancestors and for that reason are often grouped together as reptiles. They have well-developed lungs and thick skin protected by hard scales. Reptiles produce eggs with sturdy, leathery shells that can be safely laid away from water.

Birds are covered in feathers, and most can fly. They have more complex brains than reptiles, amphibians, or fish. Birds have lightweight bones and strong breast muscles for flight. They have beaks, rather than mouths full of teeth. The many varieties of birds include finches, parrots, and geese. A few, such as penguins and ostriches, cannot fly.

Adult blue jays (Cyanocitta cristata) *bring back food for their young.*

An Australian freshwater crocodile (Crocodylus johnstoni) *can grow to be three meters long.*

Both birds and dinosaurs have a particcular hole in their hip bones that no other animals have. Because of this unique characteristic, scientists think that dinosaurs are the ancestors of birds.

Mammals also evolved from a reptilian ancestor. They all have varying amounts of hair covering their skin. Most bear live babies, and all drink milk from the mother's mammary glands. They have efficient lungs and hearts, and the most complex brains of any living creatures. Mammals are extremely varied. Except for a few aquatic species— including whales, seals, walruses, and manatees— they live on land. Some eat plants, some eat animals, and others eat both. They have teeth for biting and

African elephants (Loxidonta africana) are the largest living land mammal.

chewing. Some have hooves—including horses, camels, and rhinos. Others have claws—such as cats, dogs, bears, and hyenas.

Humans are also mammals. We have hair, lungs, and complex brains. In fact, our brains are what allow us to learn about, classify, and appreciate the incredible diversity of life on Earth.

Giraffes (Giraffa camelopardalis) are the tallest living mammals.

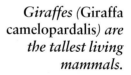

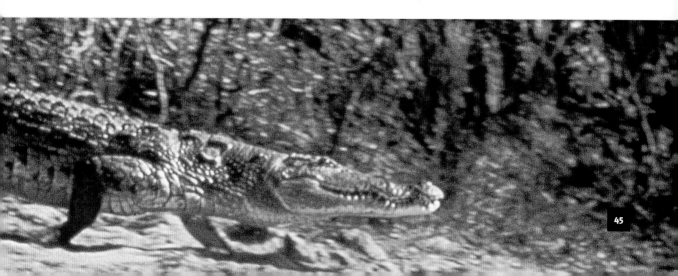

Glossary

algae A plantlike protist without roots or stems that grows in water.

amoeba An animallike protist made of one cell.

amphibian A cold-blooded vertebrate that lives in water and breathes with gills when young. Amphibians develop lungs and live on land as adults.

angiosperm A plant that flowers and fruits.

animal Any living creature that can breathe and move about.

Annelida The phylum of invertebrate animals that includes segmented worms.

archaebacteria Single-celled prokaryotic organisms that live in extreme environments.

Arthropoda The phylum of invertebrate animals that have exoskeletons, jointed legs, and segmented bodies.

autotroph An organism that makes its own food.

binomial nomenclature The naming of organisms using a two-part scientific name.

bird A warm-blooded animal with two legs, wings, feathers, and a beak.

cambium The layer of tissue between the phloem (bark) and xylem (wood) of trees.

cell The basic unit of living things.

cell membrane The thin covering of a cell.

cell wall The rigid, outer wall of most cells, not including animal cells.

chemo-autotroph An organism that makes its own food from chemicals.

chlorophyll The green substance in plants that uses light to make food from minerals, carbon dioxide, and water.

Chordata The phylum that includes all vertebrate animals.

cilia Tiny, moving, hairlike structures on the bodies of some protists.

ciliate An animallike protist that moves by fluttering its cilia.

classification The process of grouping things according to their characteristics.

Cnidaria The phylum of aquatic invertebrates whose bodies have two layers of cells.

cytoplasm The jellylike matter inside a living cell.

diatom A single-celled algae that has a cell wall made of silica.

dinoflagellate A single-celled algae that lives in the ocean.

downy mildew A funguslike protist that lives on plants.

Echinodermata The phylum of aquatic invertebrates that are protected by a thick, spiny skin.

electron microscope A large machine which uses a beam of electrons to magnify the image of an object.

enzyme A protein that causes chemical reactions to occur. Enzymes help break down food.

eubacteria A single-celled prokaryotic organism found everywhere on Earth.

eukaryotic Describes cells that contain enclosed organelles.

fern A plant with feathery leaves and no flowers. Ferns reproduce by spores.

fish A cold-blooded animal that lives in water and has scales, fins, and gills.

flagella A whiplike tail used for movement on the body of many microorganisms.

flagellate A protozoa with a whiplike tail.

fossil The trace, print, or remain of an organism preserved over time in rock.

fungus An organism digests food outside its body.

gene One part of the cells of all living things. Genes are passed from parents to offspring.

genetics The study of how characteristics are passed from one generation to another through genes.

genus A group of closely related species.

germinate In plant seeds, to begin to grow shoots and roots.

gymnosperm A seed-producing plant that does not flower.

halophile Archaebacteria that live in extremely salty water.

heterotroph An organism that cannot make its own food, but must absorb nutrients from other organims.

hornwort A non-vascular plant that grows in the shape of a horn.

invertebrate An animal without a backbone.

leaf The part of the plant that grows out from the stem and makes food by photosynthesis.

liverwort A non-vascular plant often shaped like the human liver.

mammal A group of warm-blooded animals with backbones. Female mammals produce milk to feed their young.

metamorphosis The series of changes in body shape that certain animals go through as they develop from eggs to adults.

methanogen Archaebacteria that produce methane gas.

microorganism Living things which are too small to be seen without the aid of a microscope.

microscope An instrument with powerful lenses that magnifies very small things so that they can be seen and studied.

mold A furry fungus that grows in damp places.

Mollusca The phylum of invertebrate animals that have soft bodies, a muscular foot for movement, and a mantle.

moss A kind of non-vascular plant that grows on damp soil, rocks, and tree trunks.

mushroom A fungus with fruiting bodies that are usually shaped like umbrellass.

nectar A sweet liquid in flowers that many insects, birds and bats feed on.

Nematoda The phylum of invertebrate animals that includes roundworms.

non-vascular Describes plants without tubelike structures to transport materials from one part of the plant to another.

nucleus The central organelle of a cell.

organelles Tiny structures found in the cytoplasm of eukaryotic cells.

ovary (plural: ovaries) A female organ that produces eggs for reproduction.

petal One of the outer parts of a flower that is often colored and scented to attract insects.

phloem Living tissue that transports food from photosynthesis throughout vascular plants.

photo-autotroph An organism that makes its own food from sunlight.

photosynthesis The chemical process by which green plants use energy from the sun to make their food.

pistil In flowers, a tubelike structure that leads to the ovary.

plant A multicellular organism that can make food using the sun's energy.

Platyhelminthes The phylum of invertebrate animals that includes flat worms.

phylogenetics The study of the evolutionary relationships between organisms.

pollen Tiny yellow grains that are the male cells of flowering plants.

pollinator An animal that transports pollen from one flower to another.

Porifera The phylum of the simple, invertebrate animals called sponges.

prokaryotic Describes simple cells that do not contain enclosed organelles.

protist A small eukaryotic organism that lives in wet environments.

reptile A cold-blooded vertebrate animal that crawls on the ground and reproduces by laying eggs.

rhizoid Rootlike thread on some plants that help them anchor to the soil.

root The part of a vascular plant that absorbs water and minerals from the soil.

seaweed A kind of multicellular algae that grows in the sea.

seed The part of some vascular plants from which a new plant can grow.

shoot The part of a plant that grows above ground, including the stems and leaves.

slime mold A funguslike protist that feeds on bacteria and bits of dead organisms.

species A group of organisms that have many characteristics in common.

spore The tiny reproductive body of many fungi and plants.

sporozoa A tiny, parasitic protozoa that lives in the cells of other organisms.

stamen The male reproductive organ of a flower. Stamen produce pollen.

stem The long main part of a plant from which the leaves and flowers grow.

taxonomy The study of the rules for naming and classifying organisms.

thermophile The kind of archaebacteria that live in hot environments such as hot springs.

vascular Describes plants that have tubelike structures to transport

vertebrate An animal with a backbone and well-developed brain.

virus A tiny structure that can only reproduce and grow when inside living cells.

water mold A funguslike protist that grows as a cottony mass on dead algae and animals in fresh water.

xylem The tissue of vascular plants which allows water and minerals to move from the roots up through the plant.

yeast Single-celled fungi which carries out the processes used in baking.

Index